THE DEAD GET BY WITH EVERYTHING

Poems by
Bill Holm

Other Books by Bill Holm

BOXELDER BUG VARIATIONS
THE MUSIC OF FAILURE
COMING HOME CRAZY: An Alphabet of China Essays

The Dead Get By with Everything

Poems by Bill Holm

Milkweed Editions

THE DEAD GET BY WITH EVERYTHING

Printed in the United States of America.
Published in 1991 by *Milkweed Editions*
Post Office Box 3226
Minneapolis, Minnesota 55403
Books may be ordered from the above address.

ISBN 0-915943-55-7

Publication of this book is made possible by grant support from the Literature Program of the National Endowment for the Arts, the Cowles Media/Star Tribune Foundation, the Dayton Hudson Foundation for Dayton's and Target Stores, the First Bank System Foundation, the General Mills Foundation, the I.A. O'Shaughnessy Foundation, the Jerome Foundation, the Minnesota State Arts Board through an appropriation by the Minnesota Legislature, the Northwest Area Foundation, and by the support of generous individuals.

Library of Congress Cataloging-in-Publication Data

Holm, Bill, 1943-
     The dead get by with everything / Bill Holm.
          p.   cm.
     ISBN 0-915943-55-7 : $8.95
     I. Title.
     PS3558.03558D4   1991
811'.54—dc20   90-26153
                                                                      CIP

The author is happy to acknowledge previous publication of some of these poems in the following magazines, anthologies, and books:

Magazines: *Crazy Horse, Grain, Great River Review, Iceland Review, Lögberg-Heimskringla, Milkweed Chronicle, The Nation, North Stone Review, Painted Bride Quarterly, Plainsong, Poetry Outloud, Spoon River Quarterly, Tempest.*

Anthologies: *Common Ground* (Dacotah Territory Press), *Poets of Southwestern Minnesota* (S.M.A.H.C.).

Books: *Brahms' Capriccio in C Major, Opus 76, No.8* (Oxhead Press); *The Music of Failure* (Plains Press); *Warm Spell* (Westerheim Press).

A man is lucky if he finds even one friend in a lifetime
who values him enough to tell him the truth.
I have been a very lucky man, indeed.
This book is for two who helped more even than they knew,
and who go on giving a hand, one from the next world, and one from this.
Sometimes it's hard to tell the difference.
With love and gratitude:

for Alec Bond 1938-1985
and for John Rezmerski

The Dead Get By with Everything

1
Genealogy

2
A Circle of Pitchforks

3
Traveling West

4
Learning Icelandic

5
Black Duck Love Song

6
The Dead Get By with Everything

7

Let Everything Sing Together

And I always thought: the very simplest words
Must be enough. When I say what things are like
Everyone's heart must be torn to shreds.
That you'll go down if you don't stand up for yourself,
Surely you see that.

— Bertolt Brecht, from *The Collected Poems*

1
GENEALOGY

Genealogy

When Jona at sixty traveled
to her father's farm in Iceland,
the relatives looked down
at bony knuckles, veins
popping up, said: "See!
She has the Josephson hands
even after a hundred years."

Nobody in Bill Holm's house
dared attack Franklin Roosevelt;
when the Republican uncle poked
fun at F.D.R., my father would bellow:
"You crooked son of a bitch!"
"See," they said, "there it is:
that insufferable Gislason arrogance."

Now, when I bellow at parties,
or look down at my own hands;
knuckles growing, veins
rising as I age, I think:
I'll be living with all
these dead people inside me.
How will I ever feed them?
They taught me, dragging carcasses
a thousand winters across
the tundra inside their own bodies.

Old Family Pictures

I

Great-great grandmother Gislason
looks fiercely out
under her Icelandic bonnet,
an owl who just discovered
she is a mathematical prodigy —
This is not a woman
to be monkeyed with!

II

Great-great grandfather Gislason
points toward the earth
with his whole body;
his long white beard,
a sad Old Testament prophet's
who no longer believes in God,
seems made of lead, not hair.
The farmer's shoulders,
the great heavy nose
droop . . .

He has accepted the unfairness
of the universe with good humor.
He lives with
Great-great grandmother Gislason.

Icelandic Graveyard, Lincoln County

A woman and I go to the immigrant graveyard
on top of a bare and windy prairie hill.
She's never been here, but she sees
her own name on every headstone:
Svanhilder, Svandís, Svanhvít, the swan
who died sometimes an old lady flocked
by children, grandchildren, great-grandchildren,
petals grown up around a flower.
Sometimes she died a child who couldn't talk,
gone away without God's water on her head.
Sometimes the name spelled right, sometimes not.
It's good to die so many times, she says,
to feel the death shuddering in your bones
so often; when muscles practice this well
they move with a dancer's delicate grace.

Round Barn, Westerheim

She and I go out to the round red barn
by the river; it smells of old hay; wind
slides through the missing shingles
in the high dome; empty iron stalls; hoof prints
on black dirt from cattle long dead and eaten.

She takes down from a nail an old
horse harness, leather cracked and dried.
"From Iceland," she says and caresses it.
We go into the empty hayloft, fifty feet
high, cathedral-shaped; the last light
blown into holes in the dome by prairie winds
polishes the floor to a ballroom shine.

Under the dome, I start to sing an old Italian song
about the lips of Lola the color of cherries;
the sound grows and rolls around the dome,
until it comes back transformed into horses' neighing.

Icelandic Music in Taunton, Minnesota

She and I go on Saturday night
to a noisy farmers' bar. One blind
drunk old Icelander ambles over
to talk to her. Unused to beautiful
women, shy in his drunkenness, he says
everything wrong: "Who's this, eh?
Half the time you got one who never
says a word." She leans close to his ear:
"Speak a little Icelandic to me."

Nothing comes to him but a vulgar
old song men sing when their horses
pull them home, half sleeping, in the wagon.
The horse plods down the dirt road, the voice
rises from the wagon floor in the dark:
"I was so drunk I didn't know day from night."
His father's voice, sixty years ago.
When the blond woman laughs again, he hears
his mother putting horses in the barn.

The Icelandic Emigration to Minneota, Minnesota

I

After only a thousand years where they were,
In Vopnafjördur, Floi and Jökulldal,
They left again, some for coffee, some for land,
Some no doubt for the hell of it, and came here.
They did not keep slaves, did not get capital,
Did not open any more wilderness. They farmed,
Grumbled, voted Republican, said their Rs wrong,
Dreamed in genders. A few went out to the barn
With ropes, but from another few it dropped away
So quickly that after a few years you could
Not tell them from the others. By the next
Generation the names went wrong in the neighbors'
Mouths; the R slipped off the teeth, and slid back
Into the throat. The dreams came in genders now
Only after whiskey, or when the last disease
Fastened its baling hook deep into the brain.

II

In the third generation, all that was left:
Sweet cake, small stories, a few words whose meaning
Slunk away to die under the mental stone
That buries all the lost languages in America.
The Mayans are there, Pequod and Penobscot,
And the Mandingo, and the Delaware Swedes.
The first tongue lost, did they acquire another?
The language of marketing and deterring
For the language of fish, poverty and poems?

In *The Invasion of the Body Snatchers,*
Seed pods open in your own closet at night,
Metastasizing into a body in-
distinguishable from your own, but the brain
Is something new, without memory, without
Passion, without you. Is this what it's like
To become a whole American at last?

2
A CIRCLE OF PITCHFORKS

At the Writers' Conference

After my rambunctious verbal assault
on two thousand years of Christian baggage,
three thousand of European mistakes,
a sprightly, pin-curled old lady with sad eyes
asks: "Why do you call it Christian baggage?"

This conversation can't go on. We both know it.
How do I explain in three minutes
why everything has been dead wrong
since the beginning?
Authority made of paper, strategy in vestments,
charity wearing sidearms, risen corpses,
virgin mothers, just armies . . . Damn the logic!

My baggage is her furniture; she lives
in my fire sale, serves tea every day in thin
blue porcelain cups that she imagines me
smashing one after the other
with arrogant clumsiness, tossing them into
the fearful darkness outside her parlor window.

Rose Bardal

Rose, her face pinched toward God,
used to disappear during church picnics.
The men spread out in the field until
they found her preaching in Icelandic
to the cornstalks with a loud voice.
They always brought her back before
she converted the corn
which stood unrepentant
waiting for the picker or the hailstorm.

She wrote to the Pope in 1939
demonstrating to him clearly
the error of his opinions, giving him
in calm prose, one more chance
to be a Lutheran.
Her sister found the letter
before Rose found a stamp
and hid it away,
unsealed but addressed,
until after they both were dead.
I found it, ready to go to:
MR. PIUS XII, VATICAN, ROME, ITALY, EUROPE.

Maybe I'll mail it forty years late,
see if it works, maybe the ones
to Hitler, Roosevelt, Stalin too.
While the rest of the world waited
like zombies for another mound of corpses,
this crazed woman saw God's hand
moving among corn leaves, firmly
pulling out the cockleburs.

Presidential News Conference

This face is death disguised as Grandpa,
not pitted and terrible, but affable, handsome,
a natty dresser, a good ballroom dancer.
Worst of all, it means well.
When it talks, everything you love—
moose antlers, willow bark, wind
blowing over water—disappears unless
something still animal left inside
your stomach rolls over and growls
when it comes into the room.

Paranoia

After twenty years of this,
the hell with you all!
I'm the American, not you.
Maybe I only seem to lose
all the elections myself.
I walk into a church—
membership declines.
I apply for a job—
computer learned it yesterday.
I state a firm belief—
they think it's irony.
Overhead, geese still migrate on time,
don't bother with passports,
honking for anybody
to listen, singing:
I'm the American, not you . . .
O, sing it again, goose!
You're the American, not
them. Not them. Not them.

The History of Land

First the glacier had it, then the buffalo, then the buffalo and
Sioux together. I know the facts; I've picked rocks and found
arrowheads.

Then Sveinn Johannesson got it from the Homestead Office
which didn't want it. Suddenly it had collected names and
numbers the glacier never dreamt of: "The Northwest Quarter of
Section Thirty-two in Township One Hundred and Fourteen
North of Range Forty-two West on the Fifth Principal Meridian
in Minnesota, United States of America." Or Swede Prairie
Township in Yellow Medicine County.

Then pneumonia and an April blizzard got Sveinn, and the
Globe Land and Loan Company got the land from the widow.
Then the Depression got the Globe, and Bill Holm, Sveinn's son,
got it back, and because Hitler invaded the Sudetenland, he got
it paid for.

Then a stroke got him while chasing cattle, and a new farmer
got the land, and until the First Bank System, Minneapolis, gets
it, he will probably have it.

So far it has been worth: gravelly ice ten thousand years ago,
buffalo guts and grass one thousand years ago, five years labor in
1885, fifty dollars per acre in 1910, one thousand dollars per acre
in 1925, nothing in 1930, one hundred dollars per acre in 1940,
two hundred dollars per acre in 1960, two thousand dollars per
acre in 1980, and two hundred dollars per acre in 1985. It's hard
to assess because of these fluctuations, but the county office does
its best.

I hold with buffalo guts myself, or maybe five years' work.
It's a lot like the history of America, worth both nothing and
everything.

Spring Again

Why this anger at grass or pigweed
or aphids killing honeysuckle?
This is just what happens in the world.
It's us who fertilize our own
miseries and love them.
We are a human patch of dandelions,
each yellow flower mumbling:
one more war, one more of those
presidents and then we'll stop.
Every drink is the drunk's last one,
then the next one, and the next one,
and we all know it, whatever
public lies we tell each other
while bending our heads to the hoe.

A Circle of Pitchforks

*(A poem about the farmers' protest against a proposed
powerline through Pope County, Minnesota)*

I

They used to call it a sheriff's sale.
Had one over by Scandia in the middle of the Thirties.
My dad told me how
the sheriff would ride out to the farm
to auction off the farmer's goods for the bank.
Neighbors came with pitchforks
to gather in the yard:
"What am I bid for this cow?"
Three cents. Four cents. No more bids.
If a stranger came in and bid a nickel,
a circle of pitchforks gathered around him,
and the bidding stopped.
Even in the gray light of memory
the windmill goes around uneasily,
the farmer's overalls
blow into the fork tines,
the striped overalls look like convict suits.
A smell of cowshit and wet hay seeps into everything.
The stranger wears tweed clothes
and a watch chain.
The sheriff's voice weakens
as he moves from hayrack to hayrack
holding up tools,
describing cattle and pigs
one at a time.

The space between those fork tines
is the air we all breathe.

II

"Resist much, obey little."
Walt Whitman told us.
To bring the light!
That's the thing!
Somewhere in North Dakota
lignite gouged out of the prairies
is transformed into light.
But you are not in darkness, brothers,
for day to surprise you like a thief.
We are all sons of the light,
sons of the day;
we are not of the night,
or of darkness.
Let us not sleep, as others do
but keep awake and be sober.
Those who sleep,
sleep at night,
and those who get drunk,
are drunk at night.

III

There is so much light in Minnesota:
the white faces brought here from Arctic Europe,
the lines of white birch in the white snow,
white ice like a skin over the water,

even the pale sun seen through snow fog.
White churches, white steeples, white gravestones.

Come into an old cafe
in Ghent, or Fertile, or Holloway.
The air is steamy with cigarette smoke and frozen breath,
collars up under a sea of hats pulled down.
You can hardly see the mouths moving under them.
The talk is low, not much laughing.
Eat some hot dish, some Jello,
and have a little coffee and pie.
These are the men wrecking the ship of state—
the carriers of darkness.
Up in the cities
the freeway lights burn all night.

IV

My grandfather came out of Iceland
where he took orders from the Danes and starved.
After he died, I found his homestead paper
signed by Teddy Roosevelt,
the red wax still clear and bright.
In the corner, a little drawing of a rising sun
and a farmer plowing his way toward it.
A quarter section, free and clear.
On his farm he found arrowheads
every time he turned the soil.
Free and clear. Out of Iceland.
In the thirties, the farm was eaten by a bank
thrown back up when Olson

disobeyed the law that let them gorge.
In high school they teach
that Hubert Humphrey was a liberal
and Floyd Olson is a highway.

V

Out on the powerline barricades,
the old farmers are afraid their cows'
teats will dry up after giving strange milk,
and their corn will hum in the granary all night.

They have no science, no words, no law,
no eminent domain
over this prairie full of arrowheads and flowers,
only they know it,
and the state does not.

We homestead in our bodies too,
a few years, and then go back
in a circle
faster than the speed of light.

3
TRAVELING WEST

Spring Walk around a Swede Prairie Slough

I

I saw this muskrat house before,
on a cliff a thousand feet
above the sea in Ireland.
A saint lived in it there,
not a muskrat. He prayed alone.

II

Why the heap of fish bones,
the smell of wet fur
a thousand years old?
Why does wind blow in Latin now
over the wattles at Conly's slough?

III

You never see anything right
until you see it twice:
once in this world, once
more in the other one.

Under Holdrege, Nebraska

I skip stones into billowing Nebraska wheat
as if it were a rolling golden ocean.
One nips the beard in seven arcs until
it cuts into a breaker and sinks.
No telling how far that stone will drop.

Driving from Boulder to Hanksville, Utah

The moon looks like this after a long drought. A yellow highway sign with a black cow silhouette says: Open Range. For five miles in any direction: bare petrified gravel piles, gray as a dead face, not a grass blade, not a sage brush, not even a cactus.

Coming over a rise, I see one white face cow by the roadside, just watching, not eating. All this is mine, the cow must think: my range, my kingdom, my dinner . . . master of all I survey.

Yet, if there are cow dreams, that cow dreams Wisconsin: a gentle hill thick with damp grass, a glacial pothole full of almost ice water, a red barn stuffed with musty alfalfa.

But this is a Mormon cow, one of the twelve lost tribes of cow, eating her way through the meadows of Zion, grazing this bare gray gravel, empowered to dine at last on the spiritual grass that springs from the rocks in this moony tabernacle of cow.

Still, she might take a ride with me to the Midwest, where the range is closed, and where the dour farmers give up on Zion every winter, give up imagining the Kingdom of God come anyplace but somewhere else.

Torrey, Utah: Gateway to Capitol Reef Park

In Torrey, Utah, the Schwan's truck pulls up to the Shell station.
It's filled with microwave-ready sandwiches and Tombstone pizzas
frozen to cardboard bottoms. Those sandwiches were assembled
down the road from my home: Minneota, Minnesota, like
Torrey, a lonesome place in America, by farm wives, for $3.35 an
hour. Marv Schwan is my neighborhood millionaire, and since
this is America, part of what I am is part of what he is, for better
or worse, as they say in the ceremonies.

"You know Marv?" I ask the blond, straight arrow trucker.

"Just come from Marshall," he says. "First time up there. Got
trained for two weeks. Still snowing in April. Never did see old
Marv."

"Me neither."

Torrey is a hundred Mormons at the bottom of a dry gulch
ringed by red rock. Minneota, a few thousand miles north and
east is a damp, cold, tall grass cornfield.

"That Marv—he's got him quite the operation."

"He does—indeed."

Marv Schwan, who swathes icy hamburgers and pizzas with
plastic wrap and orders them trucked across the continent, is the thin
thread that binds the two of us as countrymen together, while red
dust swirls around our tires and grits our eyes and noses.

Sin in Utah

—for Jan and Dave Lee

In Utah, it is probably illegal
even to think it, much less commit
whatever it was, though in this
great emptiness of canyons, you will
probably get by with it
for a while—if nobody sees;
but if you don't do it, as Joe Hill
almost certainly didn't, they will still
shoot you for it, and music
to the contrary, you will then
be dead, or if you did it partly
and partly didn't, like John D. Lee,
the Mormon massacrer and ferry man,
they will try you once and let you off,
and a quarter century after
it has made any difference,
try you again, and hang you
for it; in Utah even not
thinking about it may not save you,
so you might as well do it. Most do.

Grand Canyon of the Colorado

This big emptiness is the hollow under
your bed at three years old where something
too fast for light waits to chew at you.

It's the hole under the pasture that cows
know about before a tornado. At night,
there's an invisible river a mile underfoot.

Watch the tourists, brave with cameras
at sundown, cowering away from the silence
flooding up at them through the dark.

Here we're all children waiting on a branch
for the sound of something climbing up
from the hole nothing should ever get out of.

The Decline of the Colorado

At Yuma, a retired accountant with prostate trouble
could piss across the Colorado.
"Used to be in the canyon business,"
the river whispers, squishing
along between cottonwoods,
"before I moved to California
to grow organic lettuce."

What does a man say to a river
that couldn't flood a ballpark after
a hundred thunderstorms?
Old geezer, it doesn't help—
my weeping for you.

Wolf Song in Los Angeles

Hear it
echo down the canyons of Wilshire Boulevard.

Four hundred and four dire wolf skulls
rinsed out of the La Brea tar pits
float in a pool of pale yellow light.

The sign says: "All different wolves."
Each empty socket a feather narrower,
skulls peculiar as fingerprints,
pickled in this muck ten thousand years.

They all look alike to me, the same wolf
trapped in tar, howling the same last song
four hundred and four times to make it
perfect. Listen carefully . . .

Thinking about American Foreign Policy on the Oregon Coast

Whatever the Law says, America ends
at the sea. This: invaded Panama
with rock and roll and night parachutes.
That: did not invade anything
except the sea caves under the cliff.
The golden sea lions laze on black
rocks, spying with big eyes, noting
troop movements on the coast road,
low tide strollers. They carry
no papers. This rock is their embassy,
the corps diplomatique from the surf.
Violate their house; they slide off
into rollers in a twinkle of whiskers,
bob up and down, open-eyed in native water,
watching you watch and listen to the boom
of sea music played day and night.
Come into this universe, they say,
where anything can happen.

Losing My Billfold in Oregon

I keep losing my billfold; first in a crayfish bar in Portland. The money is gone, but the cards come back, turned in to a cop on a commuter train. My friends think I should be happy at this odd good luck, but instead, I'm a little melancholy. It's me I'm probably trying to lose . . . I'm nearing fifty now, have been Bill Holm long enough. Without money, I can't buy anything, but suddenly now I want nothing I have to pay for. Without cards, I'm nobody except who I say I am, and that can change—all change in an eye blink.

A few days later walking down a long beach between the Oregon dunes and the noisy Pacific surf, I feel in my pocket. Gone again! Maybe I threw it to the sea when I wasn't looking. Better the tide should have it . . . Rent a car, buy dinner, have a good time with my stone in its pocket. I didn't even know until now how little I wanted that wallet, that life in America, until the sea helped me understand by being something else, clear and loud.

Whale Breathing: Bartlett Cove, Alaska

—for John Allen

A fifty foot trombone blows
under the sea a mile away.
The black horn dives
into its own music,
the spout of its sounding
shooting up after.

That noise left
a visible ghost. The whale
that made it dines
on shrimp so small
a helping would fit
on a fingernail.

Playing a grand piano now,
I want to skim from the sea
something delicate enough
to let air between strings
rise, filling the room,
let music be visible
as whale breathing.

4
LEARNING ICELANDIC

Learning Icelandic

> For a week I say nothing,
> understand only a little.
> Without words, I'm lighter;
> float around more
> than I have for years.
> Give me an order . . .
> I'll walk away,
> over the cliff, smiling.

Summer Sunday in Seydisfjördur

Long silence in this Icelandic farm kitchen;
the Last Supper carved in skin
gathered all afternoon around the table
to drink just ten more drops of coffee,
clean up cake crumbs one by one.
Everyone asks no one once or twice
if it's time yet to cut the hay.
This only starts silence again
broken apart by in-sucking breath
and *yow-yow* once in a while.
Nobody knows what to affirm, but they
affirm it anyway as if to affirm
the habit of affirming something.
We all look out the window, wait
for cold Atlantic fog to swallow up
the basalt mountains one more time,
leave a blank sky over the sea.
You can still see two rock arms
opening up at the mouth of the fjord.
I want to shout: Europe is out there!
The Last Supper wants to listen;
but no one says anything as fog
folds the fjord into itself again.

The Icelandic Language

In this language, no industrial revolution;
no pasteurized milk; no oxygen, no telephone;
only sheep, fish, horses, water falling.
The middle class can hardly speak it.

In this language, no flush toilet; you stumble
through dark and rain with a handful of rags.
The door groans; the old smell comes
up from under the earth to meet you.

But this language believes in ghosts;
chairs rock by themselves under the lamp; horses
neigh inside an empty gully, nothing
at the bottom but moonlight and black rocks.

The woman with marble hands whispers
this language to you in your sleep; faces
come to the window and sing rhymes; old ladies
wind long hair, hum, tat, fold jam inside pancakes.

In this language, you can't chit-chat
holding a highball in your hand, can't
even be polite. Once the sentence starts its course,
all your grief and failure come clear at last.

Old inflections move from case to case,
gender to gender, softening consonants, darkening
vowels, till they sound like the sea moving
icebergs back and forth in its mouth.

Vietnamese Cooking in Reykjavík

> —*for Teng Gee and Jón*

(When the boat people arrived at the airport in
Iceland, the Icelandic Red Cross gave them one red
rose and a new Icelandic name to memorize. The
Immigrants carried these cards with them at all
times to remind them.)

He is half my size, tight olive face,
a quick body, called Gunnar
in this new place, a name
he neither can remember
nor pronounce. He sways
in front of garlic, rubbing off
dry skin, whacking the bud
with a flat knife. "For juice,"
he says brokenly, and smiles.
He knows what his name is
though he carries
GUNNAR, in block letters
in the pocket of his Red
Cross corduroy pants.

Wok oil smokes. His two knives
work the garlic, mincing it
into snow. It bounces
in boiling oil. He nods.
Next come tiny haystacks
of onion, cabbage, pork, shrimp;
he trims a woody broccoli stalk,
the last of an Icelandic garden.
"This no good," he points,

"but *this* good." Pale green
broccoli soon is paper-thin
under his knives. To women
you love you could write:
"You are beautiful," in delicate
calligraphy on these pale
leaves of broccoli paper. He looks
into the pan, knows he has invented
something beyond language.

We mumble to each other thanks
and praise in Icelandic pidgin.
What a strange earth! To slide us:
immigrant and emigrant into this
arctic kitchen, then give us only
food for words; one language gone,
the other not yet born, the third:
mingling boiled fish smells
with sesame, coriander, garlic.
Outside, a mean-tempered wind
slices over the Denmark Strait,
blows the sea under the door jamb,
cold, salt, and bitter; water
that carries us wherever
we drift on earth, and back again.

Hafnarfjördur Fish Meal Plant

A gray Sunday at the beginning of winter, the sun gone down by
4:00, but the plant still working, sending up long gray shafts of
fish smoke into the twilight.

We walk through a bin of fish carcasses, half rotted. A
tractor with a loader pushes into the oozy pile and takes another
bucket to pour into the boiler.

Inside the plant, it is hot, and the smell hits you like an
octopus made of wet cement, wrapping itself around your head.
Even the ends of your hair and your fingers smell of it. A boiler
the size of a house moves around and around, attached to heavy
black chains smothered in grease that drips off into the gutters.

The boiler is alive with fire. You see it through the cracks,
the rotten fish dancing up and down in great clumps to the music
of the iron chains. A skinny old man with his hat pulled down
and greasy black rubber boots stands at the side. His face looks
made with a hatchet, cheeks gouged out, nose sliced off clean,
long wavy scar that starts under the eye and snakes back toward
the point of the ear. He looks like he lives here, sleeping under
the rolling boiler, the stink of the fish sharpening his nose, the
heat baking the juice out of him, so that the skin sinks back and
tightens on the bone. He is on his way to fish meal himself; to
be blended with oats to fatten the pigs of Norway, pure meat and
bone down to a powder at last. You wonder what you yourself
would smell like, rolled around in that cavernous boiler for a
night, skin, blood, bone, organs boiled into a gray mush, finally
dried into the fine powder that sifts through air into the pockets
of your coat, the fingers of your gloves, down the hair follicles,
inside the skin.

You go out into the snow, and the snow smells of it; you sit
in a velvet chair in an elegant house days later and rest your
chin in your hands, and the smell comes up to you, bringing

with it the music of the huge black iron chains clanking brokenly around the belly of the boiler while the burning clumps of fish guts fall from side to side like hammer strokes on an iron drum, and the hatchet-faced old man dances around, the canyons in his cheeks lit by the flaming fish.

5
BLACK DUCK LOVE SONG

Advice

Someone dancing inside us
has learned only a few steps:
the "Do-Your-Work" in 4/4 time,
and the "What-Do-You-Expect" waltz.
He hasn't noticed yet the woman
standing away from the lamp,
the one with black eyes
who knows the rumba
and strange steps in jumpy
rhythms from the mountains of Bulgaria.
If they dance together,
something unexpected will happen.
If they don't, the next world
will be a lot like this one.

Warm Spell

A long November warm spell;
all the blizzards still asleep.
Bees hum unbelieving
around still blooming flowers.
Leaves, piled in compost heaps,
move around uneasily.
The dried branch bends down
in warm wind,
inviting them home again.

People who haven't spoken in years
smile and greet each other in the street.
Relatives forget old quarrels
over family heirlooms.
The town atheist admits that God exists;
and the town drunk drinks coffee on his porch.
The Lutheran minister forgets
St. Paul and the furrows
vanish from around his mouth.
Children are conceived in the open air
under willow trees by the river.

Like the life in the body,
this cannot last, so everyone
wastes time joyfully,
not even remembering
the old wounds they gave their spirit.
The old man on the stoop
in front of the beer joint
remembers his first lover,
and his toes begin dancing
around inside his shoes.

Weather

Early November in Minnesota.
Warm bright days, clear nights —
everyone knows what's coming
so their faces glow
like the fading pictures of saints in old churches.
Cattle lie down in long rows
in the feed lot, stare
silently at the sunlight, licking
each other now and then
with long rough tongues.

I feel that tongue now —
a river of sand moving up and down my back.
I want to make love on a grassy hill,
no one but cows for miles around;
no sound but mooing and wind in grass;
dance under the boxelder tree;
leap and splash in the river:
a hungry old carp catching flies.

The afterlife must be like this —
a gift I stopped waiting for
that suddenly came, so I praise
dark-eyed women; hillsides
full of blood-red rose hips,
nights so clear stars count
each other, glow like golden
nails in a polished ebony board.

Soup

I come back to my house after seeing her,
this lover of ladybugs, stones, and weeds.
In the refrigerator, I find the bones of a duck,
a little meat still clinging here and there.
Into the iron pot I put the duck,
dried peas, onions, carrots, wine,
prairie sage picked in November sun
from meadows next to Lac Qui Parle.
As I shred the sage, geese begin to honk,
flying low over treetops, gold light
glowing though their wings. Soon
the iron pot boils, and the house
fills with the smell of soup.
I remember the feeling of this woman,
her hands, this pot of soup,
the rush of white tails through the bare woods,
black vines hanging from the boxelders—
the heart swinging back and forth in the body.

Sparrows

Morning after first snow —
outside my kitchen window,
gray sparrows flap up
and down on a sagging clothesline.
It is a corn dance
in honor of sunshine on snow.

What joy in a sparrow's body
as he jumps and eats —
a world of red barns,
snow, old clotheslines
and corn kernels is enough.
No brooding on hunger and death,
no suspicion among the sparrows.

I return from seeing a woman,
full of joy and dancing in my body —
lie awake all night
putting away old dreams like a man
packing for a long trip.

Now it is clear: her face
comes to me, and I sink
into sleep like childhood,
rising hours later to bright sun,
sparrows dancing on the clothesline.

In a world of grief, no one
has any right to such gifts
as I am given; I take them,
put on my feathers, and go
dance on the snow.

Noises

January. I lie sleeping
in this apartment bedroom next
to the woman I love.
I wake: muffled gunshots,
hailstones cracking windows.

She sleeps. It must be trolls who
heard I was happy, rented rooms
in my dreams. No. These are the rafters
at thirty below, contracting
for the night, settling, groaning.

Already I know
she will leave,
know also
my body will make
these noises when
it finally happens.

Shoes

I find the tiny shoes
you left in my house,
put them next to my own,
imagine your naked feet
slipping under covers,
late at night still
cold from the floor
and touching mine.
A shiver slips from my body
out past the bed post
through the window, into the night.

Lilacs

In May, lilac blooms
outside the open door.
I stagger around
my kitchen; I am
a hermit saint aroused
from dreams of naked women,
barely awakened.
Air purple and smoky
with its smell: the musk
of a woman after making
love—the smell of lilacs.

Stone

He dreamed of beautiful women,
but every real one was flawed or
found some flaw in him,
so he reached the middle of his life
waking every morning to feel
some part of himself turned to stone.

Sometimes a toe, or a corner of an ear,
or a heart valve; on bad mornings
a finger, or a whole hand.
He lay in bed thinking the only thing
left was to join a traveling show.

In a tent, great crowds could gather
to watch organs turn to stone,
the audience making loud bets:
"Five dollars says it's an arm."
"Give you ten on the liver."
"Watch the cock, it's going now!"

He trembled in his bed wondering
what sort of universe he was born into.
But every morning sunlight came
through the bedroom window.
The air was loud with birds.
Dried oak leaves rustled in the spring wind.
Squirrels leaping bent and swayed high branches.

The universe seemed to be doing
perfectly all right for itself.

Black Duck Love Song

—for John and Lorna Rezmerski

The sign in front
of the fiberglass duck
in the Black Duck Park
reads: "Keep off the Duck."
I don't. Part of the world
is like that. Someone
makes something odd.
Someone else puts up
a sign that says:
"Don't finger the bread.
Don't squeeze the tissue.
Keep off the grass.
Break it and you bought it."

Some people don't pay
any attention to signs;
touch each other anyway,
bend, chip, maybe break,
ride black duck wings
onto the statue's eyebrow,
hang glide illegally down
into the canyon they
never noticed before,
handling each other in
the most remarkable way.

6
THE DEAD GET BY WITH EVERYTHING

Reading Alone in Minneota Late at Night

In September, the dark comes back to stay
for a long time. I notice it
lying around the house just before
what ought to be dawn.
In a couple of months, these corners
fill entirely up with half
eaten light, spiders doing their best
to sew it up once and for all.

Old Sow on the Road

—for Walt Gislason

Thirty below. A hundred miles from home
the Buick throws a rod. Dead.
An hour later, I'm headed south
away from Paynesville in a truck.
A half mile out an old sow sits
on broken haunches in the middle
of the road. We stop. Maybe
fell off a stock truck: nobody
saw her in the iced-up mirror.
She swivels on that broken back, a pink
lazy Susan turning on the yellow line.
Ice blue light, gun barrel pavement,
pink nose, snow, snow, more snow.
Airy colors for such a monster painting.
Windows iced tight, heater purrs loud,
but by God, I hear the howling
of that old sow, snout rotating, a double
barreled gun aimed straight at me.
And that face! That face said everything
I'll ever say until I'm either dead
or alive as that sow at that moment
wanted so badly to be.

Turtle

I

After the turtle was long dead,
body roasted and eaten, head
buried in a shallow grave, a dog
dug it up, found jaws
opening, closing, powerful enough
to bloody his nose.

II

Hindus imagine the world held
delicately on trunk tips
of four elephants standing on
an ancient turtle's back.

Turtle is the oldest life,
has no intention of evolving
toward anything; therefore
is mother of everything.

Turtle celebrates love with
a long joyful roaring that is
a god's voice inside him.

Scientists don't know
how long he lives, quite
how he dies. Good.

III

Look into a snapping turtle's eye
who suspects you are about to eat him.

A turtle in Wilno, Minnesota,
dined on chickens in a farmer's yard,
reaming them apart with pincer gums.
The blood and feather trail
lead to the pond.

"Wally," the farmer said,
"you eat turtle;
come get him."

IV

At Wally's Wilno tavern
Adeline says, "Got a big snapper
out back, over thirty pounds."

"Can I see him?" I ask.

We walk behind the barroom.
With a five gallon pail
she dips water from a barrel:
"You can see him better now."

Wally sticks a two by four
into the barrel. A neck shoots
from the gnarled shell;
jaws grab at air.

I would lie if I said
we understood one another,
but he wanted my hand,
and I think I loved him;
white claws, finger size,
gouged on the board;
leather muscles taut
at joints, tongue shot
out in silent howling.

V

"He'll be a bastard to kill," she says.
"I'll hold out a piece of meat
and when he goes for it,
Wally'll get the head in a pincers
and I'll saw it off at the neck.
But he won't die yet!
Damn things live without the head!
We nail him to a tree and bleed him
twelve, fourteen, sixteen hours;
kill him at night—By God!
next morning those claws will
still be grabbing out at you.

"So I pull the claws out, skin him;
he'll dress out about twenty pounds;
soak him a day or two in salt water;
brown him in a little butter and flour
and roast him in a big pan."

VI

Uninterested in words
turtle says nothing.

VII

An old Indian had a snapper
who searched out drowned bodies like
a truffle pig snuffling under an oak.
He'd row to the middle of the lake,
drop the snapper with wire
coiled to its thorny tail;
when the wire snapped taut
they rowed straight to the body.

VIII

Turtle saw dinosaur thump
on earth, pulled
inside his ribs, waiting
for something to change.

After a hundred million years
when thunder lizards lie
pickled in fossil beds,
turtle still opens his box,
puts out his head

into the smoky air.
If he sang, he'd sing:

"Size did not suffice;
fur got you nowhere.
Patience of soul,
not power, survives.
My box filled
with light—"

IX

This is not a riddle.
Turtle is turtle;
will clip off your finger
if you doubt it.
But he is the dead, too,
who will not let go,
poke out their heads
from under our hard
body at all
the strangest hours.

The Dead Get By with Everything

—for Alec Bond 1938-1985

I

I talk to the dead in the middle of the night
raising my voice when they don't answer.
Maybe they speak a foreign language now.
I feel like an old Spaniard shouting at a Mayan,
asking over and over on what strange shore I'd landed,
while he stands mute and ironic
in the presence of a crescendo of gibberish.
No wonder the old explorers killed everything
that wouldn't speak to them in their own tongue.

II

Dead on Wednesday,
classes as usual Thursday,
clean the office Friday;
a new job to advertise
since you gave up tenure
for this unexcused leave of absence.
I suppose tenured jobs are hard
to come by in the next world too.
You should have made arrangements just in case
you may decide there's nothing smarter
there than here, and come back
to clean your office up at last.
I'd like to see what the contract
says about that, and the expression
on whatever face rummages
at your desk when you amble in,
to finish the job before departing
under boot soles and up toward sun,
disembodied, triumphant, dead.

III

It's a bad winter; snow after snow,
ice storms and gale winds between.
Far below zero, door handles crack,
car defroster clogged with ice,
still not Thanksgiving yet,
six months to mosquito hatch.
But you who hated it so much,
a Tennessee man like Sam McGee,
escaped by dying just before it all began.
You missed all these threats on your life
by not having one left to threaten.
It's your fault I feel this shivering
in the valves of my own heart.

IV

In a long dying, you eat what you love
a little at a time, a few bites a day
and when the plate goes away from the table,
empty, there's a feeling of satisfied desire.
You have finished whoever is gone
and can hear that name spoken
without weeping. You come when called,
do their business, and after a while
it all seems so easy that you add their names
to your own. You take their tax deductions,
answer their mail. When it's time to clean the closets,
you wonder why you bought clothes
that hang so strangely on your body.
You sigh and send on boxes to the starving,
who can wear out whatever life is left
in the overcoat. Meanwhile, you wear out the soul
that never got properly used up.

But with a sudden dying, it's different.
You go to bed with a full, innocent stomach,
and wake up to discover your skin's
too small for the whale you swallowed in your sleep.
You try to throw it up, but it won't come.
That dying is inside you for good.
It will be slow digesting—months, even years,
before that protein makes its way
toward where it always goes—

to the grass and the irises, the pigeons
and the snow. You moan from bloat, complain
to the sofa that you sink too far into its cushions.
Your own dog snarls at you.
Nothing can be done about this.

V

Who do the dead think they are!
Up and dying in the middle of the night
leaving themselves all over the house,
all over my books, all over my face?
How dare they sit in the front seat of my car,
invisible, not wearing their seat belts,
not holding up their end of the conversation,
as I drive down the highway
shaking my fist at the air all the way
to the office where they're not in.
The dead get by with everything.

7
LET EVERYTHING SING TOGETHER

August in Waterton, Alberta

Above me, wind does its best
to blow leaves off
the aspen tree a month too soon.
No use wind. All you succeed
in doing is making music, the noise
of failure growing beautiful.

Mozart, Saskatchewan

—for Tom Sand

In the big emptiness of short grass prairie,
Someone named this whistle-stop: Mozart.
Maybe the railroad magnate leafing
Through the dictionary of great composers?
Maybe the immigrant farmer who once
Played *Figaro* tunes on a concertina,
Continents, oceans, light years away?
Does it make any difference now?

Here in the middle of nothing stands something:
A brown elevator named Wheat Pool Mozart
With an empty boxcar under its silver tongue
Ready to carry off all the dusty music
That falls out of its mouth whenever
The market for singing comes right at last.

Ernest Oberholzer and Billy McGee Go Canoeing on Rainy Lake
    —for Gene Monahan and Allen Snowball

I

In 1913, table feet had claws, men scowled in photographs, World
Wars unnumbered yet, your grandmothers and Teddy Roosevelt
still alive. Two, one a Harvard man, the other Ojibwa, paddle
under a full May moon. Clicks and whispers rise from the just-
broken ice. Otherwise silence. The men say little. One wears
knickers and high boots, a plaid wool shirt, too hot now in
spring. The other wears a skin shirt, face dark under brimmed
hat. A fish leaps. An otter rolls over a few hundred yards ahead.
Ernest Oberholzer spots a moose shadow erect near shore, its
ancient nose pointed somewhere under water as if music were
rising from that spot. Years later, he writes about moose, saying:

> *Sooner or later you will meet one—that ludicrous*
> *patchwork of snout, hump, bell and flapping ears which*
> *the scientists say is one of the oldest animal forms, and*
> *more than looks it. He not only completes the illusion of*
> *the past; he makes the Pleistocene a reality.*

II

But now it is May, 1913, on Rainy Lake where Canada and
Minnesota come together at the bullseye of the continent. The
two canoeists have still not made camp. Billy McGee paddles
while Oberholzer reaches down in the ribs of the canoe, brings
up a violin case. He tightens the bow, rosins its hair, tunes. Bare
fifths ring over splashing fish, moose breathing. He bows a
chord—D minor. Bach's *Chaconne.* Neither moose, otter, nor
Indian know this music, though they have heard it many times

before. They listen. The violin misses notes in this spiny grandiose piece, yet sound goes swelling up from that canoe into the night, as if the canoe itself were being bowed by something invisible beside it in the water.

Not just the illusion of the past, this is the past itself, 1913 also a Pleistocene, ice still not quite gone on the cold lake, stone islands only shadows as the moon passes under a cloud, the *Chaconne* moving into a major key down in the low violin strings, the moose slowly lifting his great heavy nose up from the water into the cold spring night.

Blizzard

After midnight the blizzard howls itself out,
the wind sleeps, a tired lover.
Before bed, I think of you
and play the *Meistersinger* quintet
over and over, singing
along on all the parts,
dancing through the house
like a polar bear who thinks
it has joined the ballet.
You are in my arms, dancing too;
whirling from room to room;
frost crusted on the window
begins to glow like lit up faces.
My five fingers, now on fire
like these five voices singing,
imagine touching the skin
over your shoulders.

Scott Joplin

—for Etheridge Knight

I

He never smiled, his friends said,
but looked out at you
from those doleful eyes,
like turned-down gas lamps
set in a coal-black wall.
He did not sing
the song of the happy darkie
to set toes tapping
in St. Louis whorehouses.
The darkness within him
was darker and lovelier than
the elegant black curve of his nose—
than the smooth black hands
moving over the ivory keys—
blackbirds flying in a fog.

II

Once he had a daughter
whose dying split his heart
like a sounding board.
He spent ten years
bringing back to life
a honey-colored baby
deserted under a tree in Arkansas.
On the lines of music paper
spread out before him,
she sang forgiveness

to the crooked and the ignorant,
and taught them all together
to dance the Real Slow Drag.

III

In the few old photographs
the mouth turns down at the corners
like a beached canoe.
Perhaps he knew what would come,
brain gone, hands trembling,
silent piano waiting in the corner—
an upright coffin with teeth—
to pull him in, devour him
if he should touch it,
and spit him out, years later,
his black skin unrolling
as from a player, full
of little squares and diamonds
that are ghosts of hands.

IV

Behind the iron piano strings
his leaves and flowers—Maple Leaf,
Fig Leaf, Rose Leaf, Palm Leaf,
Gladiola and Chrysanthemum,
Pineapple and sweet Sugar Cane
bloom over and over again,
a Heliotrope Bouquet grown
in light under the darkness

of the stony Missouri ground
that he worked into music
with those elegant black hands.

Playing the Goldberg Variations on Sunday Morning

These thirty carved stones
were carried out of a Lutheran
church no longer standing.
In this church, priests
made love on the altar;
St. Paul's name was not
spoken; wine was given
in huge goblets because it was
wine, and wine is enough.
The organist played always
in G major, the same tune
slowly, and the priest mumbled
to himself: "Whoever loves
G major loves God."
From this church, buried
in rubble from one of those wars
fought for love of God,
thirty stones were saved,
in a boat pulled down a brook
by swans. No one ever named
the faces carved on those stones:
stones still wet from the river
and from swans' breathing.

Opening

In this small cabin, a man and a woman lay uneasy under
an old horse hide, a suspicious silence between them.
Roses bloom in a wash tub at the foot of the bed;
black-faced sheep stand outside the window,
moonlight floating up from their gray wool.
Horses eating and human breathing mix in a song
we always wanted to sing, the melody never clear until now,
or voices in a Bach fugue: snuffling horses, whispers,
the violin on the table—all weaving together.
Finally a door opens in the woman, and the man comes in,
leaves his own doors unguarded; there is a torrent
of words, then hands, the moon now light inside the shed,
inside violin wood, inside rose petals, inside fingers.

Brahms' Capriccio in C Major, Opus 76, No. 8

—for Marcy

All this lonesome fall I practice Brahms, mooning over a faraway woman, while my fingers twist around this constipated soulful counterpoint. Day after day of gray drizzle, both in October and inside the piano. I don't even like this music and haven't touched a note of it for years.

Tonight, I remember when I played it last; it was the melanoma ward of a huge gray hospital, a whole hallway chock full of the doomed. An old upright piano sat in the sun room, where I waited day after gray drizzly spring day for news I had already gotten inside. I had only Brahms along, and he seemed all right, so I practiced playing and grieving together, conscious of the one, avoiding the other.

Up and down the hall walked glucose bottles attached to bodies. All over those bodies, black holes in the skin sucked up life and energy, burrowing inside from eye, back, hand, cheek, slow black bullets whose trajectory stopped only when they found a brain or liver to explode.

"A nasty disease," the Chinese neurosurgeon said. "We don't know what causes it. Perhaps the sun . . . Probably the sun . . ."

Maybe gray drizzly north German counterpoint so dense the sun can't make its way inside could slow it down a little.

Without much hope for either music or survival down this hall, I practice Capriccios and Intermezzos that old Brahms probably composed while his own black holes ate at his liver. One day, I sit bungling through something in C Major when a young boy with freckles, red hair, and a glucose bottle slides noiselessly into the sun room and listens. He claps weakly when I finish, and I turn around. The glucose bottle still wobbles on its iron stand, the plastic tube trembling.

He is my color, could be my brother, but he is thin, pale,

dying, and I am fat, flushed, full of angry life. "I always wanted to play the piano," he said.

"Do it!" I said. "It's a great joy to play."

"Did it take you long to play so well?" he asked.

"Oh, not long at all!" I said. "Just practice all you can."

Then with a weak excuse, I left the sun room, went and sat next to my mother's bed and wept, because I had lied, and because I knew what happened in this world as inexorably as Brahms' ruthless logical contrapuntal knots tied and untied themselves around the human ear.

For twelve years, I forgot those Capriccios and Intermezzos, and neither lied nor wept too much. But all this lonesome fall, I practice Brahms again, mooning over a faraway woman I love — no, over two women, one gone out, and the other just come in, the old grief and this new joy so alike inside this music. One brave melody in C, clear and full of leaping rhythm, rears up against a minor tune as if to say: Let everything sing together inside you, lose nothing.

Piano

He got up, dragging his heavy parts
behind him; alone at the piano, he played Chopin,
until blood ran back into his fingers, notes
sounding when he needed them,
not hating their own silence.

So this, he thought, is Chopin's wisdom:
the hand moving in these sensual ways,
as if black dots and lines on paper
were directions to make love, notes attached
to little hammers in the blood for him to strike.

Playing the *Barcarole* one day, emotion
overcame him; they would have a life
together, make joyful noise. He played
a few chords of acceptance. They had friends
in often: Flutes, singers, violins.

But sometimes the old hunger for a human
struck him like a disease,
and he was unfaithful.
It always happened the same way:
darkness, silence, turning to stone.

But when he came back to the piano,
she forgave him, they married again,
music sounding late into the night,
the mind drawn back into the hands where
it always should have been: its only home.

Thanks

This is my third book edited by Emilie Buchwald and designed by
Randy Scholes. I first felt delight, then gratitude, and finally affection
for the attention, intelligence, and taste they give to books. They do this
not because it makes them rich but for very old reasons: a sense of
honor toward writers and a love of beauty. I salute them and thank
them. I have joked publicly that Emilie is the Max Perkins of
Minnesota. It is not a joke, or, if so, a serious one. I also thank Teresa
Bonner who gives these books an audience with her energetic
intelligence.

Poets get by, as the Beatles said, with a little help from their friends,
and I want to thank those who have helped over many years with these
poems; I list them as the telephone book finds them: John Allen, Robert
Bly, M. J. Brekken, Phil Dacey, Leo Dangel, Jim Heynen, John Rezmerski.

Bill Holm was born in 1943, the son of farmers north of Minneota, Minnesota. He still lives there. He is the author of *Boxelder Bug Variations* (Milkweed Editions, 1985), a book of poems, essays and music that was staged as a performance piece by the Lyric Theatre of Minneapolis in 1988. *The Music of Failure* (Plains Press, 1985), a book of prose about Minneota, was reprinted in hardcover by Saybrook Publishing Company in 1987 as *Prairie Days*. A new edition — with more essays — will be published by Milkweed Editions in 1992 under the original title.

Holm has taught school for twenty-five years, most recently at Southwest State University in Marshall, Minnesota, from where he went as an exchange teacher to Xi'an Jiaotong University in central China. His book *Coming Home Crazy* (Milkweed Editions, 1990) describes his experience there. He was also a Fulbright professor of American literature in Iceland, the country from where his ancestors emigrated. He is an enthusiastic musician, and when life in America is dark, he spends a good deal of time at his various keyboards playing Bach, Liszt, Charles Ives, and Jelly Roll Morton. There is a copy of *Leaves of Grass* in every room in his house.

The Dead Get By with Everything *was designed
by R. W. Scholes, set in Weiss by Peregrine Publications,
and published by Edwards Brothers Incorporated.*